PROTOEVANGELIUM
OF JAMES

SAINT **SHENOUDA** PRESS

PROTOEVANGELIUM
OF JAMES

Translated by Fr Robert Nixon, OSB

With Annotations by Fr Mark St Shenouda

ST SHENOUDA PRESS
SYDNEY, AUSTRALIA

2022

PROTOEVANGELIUM OF JAMES
Translated by Fr Robert Nixon
Annotated by Fr Mark St Shenouda

ST SHENOUDA PRESS
8419 Putty Rd,
Putty, NSW, 2330
Sydney, Australia

www.stshenoudapress.com

ISBN 13: 978-0-6455543-6-6

Publisher's Introduction

In the Coptic Orthodox Church we have many traditions passed down through many centuries about the virgin Saint Mary. With many of these traditions, the average believer does not know where they originated from. However, the Coptic Orthodox Church loves Saint Mary and takes pleasure in offering her glorifications and medleys asking for her intercession for the human race. In fact, on any given Sunday psalmody the mention of the name of the virgin Saint Mary is in excess of seventy times.

Much of the information about the virgin Saint Mary is taken from this apocryphal text. We have included in the footnotes examples of parts of prayers and doxologies that have been taken from this text, whether in part or entire sentences. Similarly, when required, we have highlighted some similarities and differences present in the corresponding scripture.

From this text it is obvious that the early church believed in the ever-virginity of saint Mary, which was a concept that was difficult to understand, let alone defend, and thus was unlikely to be invented by the faithful if it was not solemnly believed to be fact.

Apocryphal texts are those texts that are biblical or related writings that are not part of the accepted canon scripture. There are many reasons for texts not becoming part of scriptural canon, most of which are attributed to difficulty ascertaining the authenticity of the author. In this specific text the authenticity of the author being saint James is in question, along with the date of when it was written.

We hope that through this text we enlighten your eyes and your mind to the internal conflict and emotions that the virgin Mother must have felt through this trying time. We hope that you gain an appreciation for the texts and prayers of the church, specifically understanding where they came from. Finally we ask for the intercession of the ever-virgin saint Mary and the prayers of all the saints. Amen.

TRANSLATOR'S INTRODUCTION

The four canonical Gospels, which are universally accepted by Christians as the inspired Word of God, present a synopsis of the most essential elements of the life, death and Resurrection of Our Lord Jesus Christ. Yet, in themselves, they tell us little about the life of the Virgin Mary, or Joseph, or even the childhood and youth of Jesus himself. These omissions do not mean, of course, that those details were not wondrous and significant, but merely that they are beyond what Divine Wisdom determined as the fitting scope of the Sacred Scriptures. The canonical Gospels, despite their narrative form, are not detailed biographies, but rather eternal and sacred expressions of the Divine Word.

Nevertheless, it is a fitting expression of true love and devotion that the worshippers of Christ should be eager to learn also as much as possible about the life of Mary, the Mother of God. Of course, such details would have been well known by oral tradition in the earliest Christian communities, especially those in Palestine. The desire to preserve them in writing for future generations was a natural extension of this loving devotion. In this context, the work presented in translation here—commonly known as the Protoevangelium of James—is an extremely important document. While it is not a canonical scripture, it carefully preserves and presents the very earliest traditions. The text itself is believed to date from the second half of the 2nd century.

The very early traditions which it encapsulates are in no way inconsistent with the canonical Gospels themselves, or the information available from other reliable sources. Moreover, the liturgy of the Church and the writings of the Church Fathers draws upon, or closely corresponds with, material contained in this inspiring document.

It is pertinent to note something about the name 'Protoevangelium of James', which is the designation of the work used by scholars today. In fact, most manuscript sources do not bear this title at all, but rather 'The Book of the Birth of the Blessed Mary and the Infant Savior', or a variant thereof. The word 'Protoevangelium' simply indicates that the work describes events prior to, or overlapping with, the commencement of the Gospel narrative proper. Thus the work does not have any pretensions to being an additional 'Gospel' itself, but rather offers edifying and illuminating background to the canonical Gospels. The attribution of the work to James, who is identified as the 'Brother of the Lord', is to be found in many (but not all) of the manuscript copies.

As a non-canonical work, it is not surprising that there are a multitude of variants in the numerous extant manuscript sources. Clearly, scribes engaged in copying or translating a non-canonical work were not bound to the same degree of exactitude or word-for-word fidelity as in the books of the Bible itself. Versions of the work, or closely related variants of it, are to be found in many languages, including Greek, Latin, Syriac, Coptic, Ethiopian, Arabic and Old Church Slavonic. Unfortunately, some of these, such as the Coptic text, survive only in fragmentary form. Some manuscripts include the aforementioned attribution to James, whereas others have no identification of an author at all. A number of Latin manuscripts include an introductory letter attributed to St. Jerome, which tentatively identifies the author of the work as Matthew. Thus the Latin version(s) of the work are generally identified as the 'Gospel of pseudo-Matthew', despite the fact that some manuscripts give James as the author.[1]

The Greek version, which is certainly the oldest and primary form, is available today in several editions. The first publication of the Greek text was in the edition of Michael Neander (1565), which was reproduced in the important collection of New Testament apocrypha published by Johannes Fabricius in 1703. But a much more reliable and scholarly edition of the text, drawing on no less

---

1 The work referred to as the Gospel of pseudo-Matthew includes also various details of the childhood of Jesus, not found in the Protoevangelium of James.

than eighteen ancient manuscripts, was published by Constantine Tischendorf in 1876. The text of this Tischendorf edition was reproduced in several other collections.

In 1952, a Greek manuscript from the 3rd or 4th century (known as the Papyrus Bodmer 5) was discovered near Dishna in Egypt. This manuscript is believed to have been part of the library of the monastery of St. Pachomius, and is the earliest known copy of the work. The text was published in 1958, edited by M. Testuz. Yet, despite its antiquity, the Bodmer 5 text contains evident and somewhat crude lacunae and abridgments, and is therefore not necessarily any more authoritative than Tischendorf's text. The present translation is based primarily on the text of the Tischendorf edition. Where significant or interesting variants are to be found in the Neander/Fabricius and the Bodmer 5 texts, they have been identified in footnotes.

Notes have also been added including additional or variant details to be found in the Coptic fragments of the Life of the Virgin and the Latin Gospel of pseudo-Matthew. Since both of these works are essentially redactions or elaborations of the Protoevangelium, the details they contain may be considered as being part of the same tradition.

The translational approach adopted in this present work is one of dynamic equivalence, with every effort being made to produce a clear, coherent and reasonably idiomatic English text. Editorial insertions made in order to complete or clarify the sense of the narrative are indicated by square brackets [ ]. Scriptural references are noted wherever they assist in understanding the text, but very obvious references or correspondences to events in the canonical Gospels have not been noted.

It is hoped that this new translation of the work, together with its commentary, may help to encourage reverent meditation upon the wonders of the life of Mary, the Mother of God, and Jesus, our God and Savior; to whom be all glory forever and ever. Amen.

THE PROTOEVANGELIUM OF JAMES

CHAPTER 1

IN THE HISTORIES OF THE TWELVE TRIBES OF ISRAEL [IT IS TOLD that] there was once a certain man called Joachim, who was very rich.[1] He always brought a double measure when making his offering [to the temple], saying to himself, "My offerings shall serve to make reparation both for the sins of the whole people of Israel, and also for myself. In this way, God shall have mercy upon me!"

Now, once a great feast day of the Lord was approaching, and the men of Israel were all making their customary offerings. And amongst these was a certain man called Ruben.[2] And he confronted Joachim, and said to him, "It is not fitting for you to make an offering, because you have not given any offspring to the people of Israel!" [He said this because Joachim, though a married man, had begotten no children with his wife.[3]] And Joachim was deeply saddened.

He went away and studied the chronicles and genealogies of the twelve tribes [of Israel]. He said to himself: "I shall examine carefully the histories of the twelve tribes of Israel, and see if I am the only [righteous] man who has never been blessed with children." And he searched through the histories, and found that all the righteous men of the past had begotten offspring. And he remembered also the patriarch Abraham, and how [even though he had lived for many years without fathering any children] God had at last given him a son, Isaac, in his final days.

[After pondering on these things], Joachim was profoundly depressed. [In his sadness,] he did not return to his wife, but instead went forth into the desert. There he set up his tent, and fasted for forty days and forty nights[4]. And he said to himself, "I shall take neither food nor drink until the Lord my God shall look upon me; until then, my food and drink shall be prayer [alone.]"

Commentary

1   The Coptic fragment mentions that Joachim was also known as Cleopas. The Latin Gospel of pseudo-Matthew notes that Joachim was, by profession, a shepherd. Joachim is named abruptly without much of an introduction, we will see in this text that there are many characters that will follow in this manner, thus it was assumed that the early church knew who these characters where and therefore they did not need an elaborate introduction

2   The Gospel of pseudo-Matthew describes Ruben as a scribe of the temple. This statement spoken by Ruben saying that it is not right for Joachim to offer sacrifice because he has no offspring seems to have no bases in the Jewish tradition. However, it is seen that it offended Joachim greatly.

3   The Gospel of pseudo-Matthew states that Joachim and Anna had been married for twenty years at this point.

4   This recurring number of forty days and forty nights in fasting in the desert may be a prequel to the forty days and nights spent in the desert by the lord Jesus Christ before the commencement of his ministry. This number (40) seems to have great significance as we see in the scripture that Moses spent forty days and forty nights before he received the commandments and the prophet Elijah fasted for 40 days and 40 nights as he walked to mount Horeb.

CHAPTER 2

[MEANWHILE], HIS WIFE ANNA[5] LAMENTED FOR TWO GREAT sorrows, and mourned for two dire afflictions. She cried out, "I lament because I have become [as] a widow, [now that my husband, Joachim, has departed from me!] And I mourn also because I am without children!"[6]

Now, a great [feast] day of the Lord was drawing near. Her maid, Judith, said to her, "How long do you mean to torment your soul? A great feast of the Lord is at hand, and so it is not fitting for you to mourn at this time. But take this coronet, which the mistress of the servant-girls gave to me, and place it upon your head. I am just a servant [and so it doesn't suit me to wear], but you have the form of a queen!" But Anna replied, "Leave me be! I shall not do such a thing, because the Lord has humiliated me. But be careful—for perhaps some wicked person has given it to you, and you are now trying to make me a partaker in your guilt." Judith [was offended when she heard this], and replied, "Why should *I* [bother to] say anything to you when you refuse to listen to my voice, seeing that the Lord [Himself] has shut your womb, so that you have given no offspring to Israel?"[7]

Anna was deeply saddened [to be reminded of her childlessness. So, she re-considered Judith's suggestion,] and removed her robes of mourning, and adorned her head [with the coronet Judith had offered her]. She put on her splendid wedding garments.

At about the ninth hour [of the day][8] she went down to the garden to take a walk. And she saw a laurel tree, and sat under it. There she poured forth her prayers to the Lord, saying to the Lord God, "O God of my ancestors, bless me and give ear to my supplication, just as you once blessed the womb of Sarah, and gave to her a son, Isaac!"[9]

5   It is from this text that we derive the names of the father and mother of st Mary as Joachim and anna. Similarly we have the *"discourse of Mary Theotokos by Cyril archbishop of Jerusalem"* that introduces Joachim and anna in almost the same manner.

6   The Gospel of pseudo-Matthew notes that the Joachim and Anna had already been married for twenty years at this point. In the *discourse of Mary Theotokos by Cyril of Jerusalem* they state that they (Joachim and Anna) prayed at the temple together for a child, whether boy or girl and there they would dedicate the child to the temple. Similarly in the *discourse by Demetrius on the birth of our lord and the virgin st Mary,* they say that both Joachim and Anna (Susanna in that text) prayed in the temple and received the angelic announcement there.

7   It this chapter we see that even the words of Judith to her mistress Anna, while inappropriate, seem to highlight how sensitive the issue of being childless was to Anna.

8   i.e. 3:00pm.

9   The prayer we are introduced to here are reminiscent of that of a hysterical Hannah praying fervently with tears in the altar for a son.

CHAPTER 3

AND GAZING UP INTO THE HEAVENS, [ANNA] SAW A SPARROW'S nest in the laurel. She cried out in her heart, and said, "Woe is me! To whom may I be compared [in my grief]? Who conceived me, and what womb brought me forth into the world? For, indeed, I have become as one cursed amongst the people of Israel. They mock me and deride me, and have expelled me from the Temple of the Lord my God!

"To what may I be compared? I am not like the birds of the air, for these produce their young in your presence, O Lord. And I am not like the living animals which inhabit the land, for each of these brings forth its offspring in your sight, O Lord. Nor am I like the waters, for these also are productive and fertile before you.[10] Indeed, these waters of the sea, whether they are serene or turbulent, abound with fish, and, together with these, they sing your glorious praises. Alas for me! I cannot even be likened to the soil of the earth, for it brings forth its fruit in due time, and thus it blesses you, O Lord."[11]

10 Here Anna may be deriving her lament from the first psalm which states "he is likened to a tree planted by the river of water, which brings its fruit in due season". Thus anything that is blessed by the lord must be fruitful. Similarly, in the Coptic tradition, in every midnight chanting we pray the third hoos (canticle) known as the hymn of the three saintly youth. Here we implore all that is formed by the lord to bless the lord, praise him and exalt Him above all forever.

11 The repetition in annas lament here highlights song. It is through repetition rather than rhythm or rhyme that you can distinguish that this is a song of lament.

CHAPTER 4

[THEN—]BEHOLD!—THE ANGEL OF THE LORD [SUDDENLY] appeared before her. It said, "Anna, God has heard your prayer! You shall conceive and give birth to a child. And, [on account of this holy child], your fame will be celebrated throughout the entire world."

Anna said to the Angel, "The Lord my God lives! Whether I shall give birth to a boy or a girl, I shall dedicate the child to the Lord our God. And my offspring will serve the Lord in sacred things all the days of its life." [12]

And then suddenly two [more] angels appeared before her. They said, "Your husband Joachim is now coming to you with his flocks. For the angel of the Lord has appeared to him, and said to him, 'Joachim, Joachim, the Lord has heard your prayer! Depart from here. For your wife, Anna, shall conceive a child in her womb.'"[13]

[When Joachim had heard the angel of the Lord speak to him thus], he went down and summoned his shepherds. He said to them, "Bring to me ten female lambs which are pure and immaculate. These I shall offer to the Lord my God. And bring to me also twelve faultless cattle, and these shall be an offering for the priests, the clergy and the elders. And bring to me also one hundred goats, and these shall be an offering for all the people."

And—behold!—Joachim went forth with his flocks. Now, Anna was standing at the Gates [of the city,] and she saw Joachim coming, together with all his flocks.[14] And she rushed forth to him, and embraced him warmly around the neck. She declared joyfully, "Now I know that the Lord God has blessed me most abundantly. For I was a widow, and now I am a widow no longer! I was barren, but now I shall soon conceive a child!"[15] And Joachim took his rest in his house, for the first day [after his return.][16]

12 Anna takes the same vow as Hannah the mother of Samuel the prophet. Not knowing weather, she will bear a boy or girl. In many of the discourses (by Cyril of Jerusalem or Demetrius), it is written that both Joachim and Anna took this vow together.

13 In the Coptic church we refer to st Mary as the daughter of Joachim in many of the midnight chanting's and especially in the month of kiahk. For example in the Sunday theotokia:

   i   *Through Mary the daughter of Joachim, we learned the true sacrifice for the forgiveness of sins.*

   ii   *They called Mary the daughter of Joachim, the true tabernacle of the lord of hosts.*

14 In the Gospel of pseudo-Matthew, Anna has a vision of an angel who instructs her to wait at the Golden Gate of the city for her husband to return.

15 In the Coptic tradition we do not believe that the virgin St Mary's conception was immaculate however we believe in the immaculate conception of Jesus Christ by the virgin Mary. Therefore, it is assumed that this is the day of the conception of the virgin Mary.

16 There are many similarities in this part of the story to that of the parents of the judge Samson, in that each of the parents have an independent vision. How similar is the fact that samson will save his people from the philistines and that Mary will be the mother of Christ, who will save his people from their sins.

CHAPTER 5

THE NEXT DAY, [JOACHIM] BROUGHT HIS OFFERINGS [TO PRESENT them at the temple.] He said to himself, "If the Lord God has truly blessed me, the [golden] plate of the priest [which he wears upon his miter] shall reveal this to me."[17] So, as Joachim brought forth his offerings, he intently observed the plate [worn by the priest.] As he went up to the altar of the Lord, he looked carefully. And—behold!—there was no sin to be found in himself.[18] And Joachim said, "Now I know that the Lord has been merciful to me, and has forgiven me all my sins!" And he left from the temple of the Lord, having been made righteous [in the sight of God], and returned to his home.

And [soon afterwards] Anna conceived a child. The [first] six months [of her pregnancy] passed [without difficulty].[19] And in the ninth month Anna gave birth to her child. And she asked the midwife, "What have I delivered?" And [the midwife] answered, "It is a girl!" Anna exclaimed, "My soul exalts at this time!" And she laid the infant down.

After the appointed days had passed and she had completed the ritual of purification, Anna nursed the child. And she gave to her the name of Mary[20].

17 This is reference to the golden plate which adorned the front of the priestly miter, as described in Exodus 28:36-37.

18 This suggests that the plate worn in the priestly miter would somehow show if there was any sin in the person who was making the offering. Exodus 28:38 indicates that this plate represented the priest as bearing any iniquity which may be associated with offerings made. Precisely how this is to be understood is not clear.

19 The editorial insertions here seem necessary to complete the sense.

20 The name Mary when used in the correct Hebrew context means bitter. As was stated by Naomi after her return to the land of her father's when she had lost her husband and both sons "do not call me Naomi call me Mara (bitter)". This is the same name given to the nursing infant by her mother Anna. This may be due to the fact that after such a long time and after finally bearing a child, they will still part with her and she will be given to the temple. Likewise, if we think forward to what Simeon the elder will say to st Mary when they present the lord Jesus to the alter, he alludes to st Mary suffering bitter heart ache over her son. "Behold this child is destined for the fall and rising of many in Israel and for a sign which will be spoken against (yes a sword will pierce through your own soul also) that the thoughts of many hearts may be revealed". (Luke 2:34-35)

CHAPTER 6

THE LITTLE GIRL GREW STRONGER AS EACH DAY PASSED. WHEN SHE was six months old, her mother placed her on the floor, to see whether she was able to stand up. And she walked seven steps, and then returned to her mother's embrace. And Anna exclaimed [with joy], "The Lord my God lives! You shall not walk upon the ground, until I have taken you into the Temple of the Lord!" And she made a nursery [for Mary] in her own bedroom, and allowed nothing unclean to come into contact with the girl, and took the greatest care to keep her separated from all pollution.[21] And she summoned [to her household] the most faultless and pure daughters of the Hebrews, and these served to entertain and amuse [her daughter.]

And it came to pass that [Mary] reached her first birthday.[22] [On this auspicious occasion,] Joachim held a great celebration[23], and invited the high priests, the scribes, the elders, and all the people of Israel. And Joachim presented his child to the chief priests; and they blessed her, saying: "O God of our ancestors, bless this little child, and give her a name which will be honored by all generations!" And all the people responded, "May it be so! May it be so! Amen.[24]" And he brought her to the [other] priests. And they blessed her [too], saying, "O God of the highest Heavens, look down upon this girl-child, and bless her with a blessing which has no end!"

And then her mother took up the child into her embrace, and began to nurse her. [And as she did so,] Anna sang a song to the Lord God, saying:

21 There is great detail here about the celebration that Joachim and anna performed at receiving the child. Firstly, it is important to note that much of this was passed in oral form in the early church.

22 The fact that we discuss the childhood of the virgin Mary in such detail is a testimony to the love the early church had for her.

23 There is also massive contrast here to the postpartum of our lord Jesus Christ. Where he was born in a lowly manger (cave) and without the presence of priests and blessings, and there was no celebratory service besides that of the Hebrew ritual and sacrifice.

24 Where we see in the gospels that the priests and scribes where in constant conflict with Jesus, here we have them portrayed in a close pastoral roll with Joachim and his family.

"I shall sing the praises to the Lord, my God,
for He has visited me and taken away the
reproaches of my enemies.
The Lord God has given to me the abundant fruit
of justice in His sight.
Oh, who shall declare to the sons of Ruben[25] that
I, Anna, now nurse a child?
O hear, hear, you twelve tribes of Israel that Anna
[who once seemed barren] now nurses her child!"

And then, [having completed this canticle of praise], she laid the child to rest in her nursery. [Anna] then returned [to her guests] and served them. Once the feast had reached its end, everyone went home filled with the greatest joy, glorifying the God of Israel.

25 This seems to be a reference to the same Ruben, the
scribe of the temple, who prevented Joachim from
making his offering in the temple, on account of his
lack of offspring.

CHAPTER 7

[AS TIME WENT BY,] MONTHS WERE ADDED TO [THE AGE OF] THE child. And when [Mary] had reached the age of two years, Joachim said to his wife Anna, "Let us present [our daughter] in the Temple of God, so that we may fulfil the vows which we have promised. For otherwise, the Lord may turn His face away from us and our offering may become unacceptable to Him." But Anna replied, "Let us wait until she is three years old, lest she [should become distressed,] seeking after her father and mother!" And Joachim [agreed to this, and] said, "[Very well.] Let us wait [for another year.]"

And when the child was three years old[26], Joachim said, "Summon [to our household] the most faultless of the daughters of the Hebrews. Let them each take lamps and let these lamps be lighted. [They shall accompany our daughter, Mary, as she goes to the temple, so that] she shall not turn back, nor her mind be diverted from the Temple of God[27]." And thus it was done, until [Mary and the maids who escorted her] had entered the temple. And the high priest accepted the child[28]. He kissed her and said, "Mary, the Lord has magnified your name in all generations! In these last days, the Lord will reveal His redemption to the people of Israel." He sat her upon the third step of the altar, and the Lord God sent his grace down upon her[29]. Immediately she sprang up and danced for joy. And the whole house of Israel loved her.[30]

26 Joachim and anna hastened to fulfill their vow to the lord, and as such we are informed that the virgin Mary was living in the temple from the age of 3.

27 It seems as though this was a common tradition as Mary was not the only young virgin dedicated to the service of the temple from such a young age.

28 *The discourse on Mary Theotokos* by Cyril of Jerusalem he states that Joachim and anna visited her once each month and brought her anything of which she may need.

29 The author here highlights the fact that at the tender age of three, Mary did not turn back and look for her parents, this seems highly unnatural, however it may allude to the life of devotion that st mary will come to live and brings to memory her famous quote "behold the maidservant of the lord, let it be to me according to your word"(Luke 1:38)

30 The Coptic fragment of the *Life of the Virgin Mary* states that her face began to grow with a brilliant light at this time. There is much contrast here to the story of Samuel the prophet who was handed to Eli the priest as soon as he was weaned, he too was vowed by his mother into the service of the Lord.

CHAPTER 8

HER PARENTS THEN LEFT [THE TEMPLE,] MARVELING AND PRAISING God. [Indeed, they were very surprised] because the child had not turned back towards them [as they departed]. And Mary, like a gentle dove, abode in the Temple of the Lord. There, she accepted food from the hand of an angel.[31]

But when she reached the age of twelve years,[32] there was a council of priests held in the Temple of the Lord. [They deliberated amongst themselves,] "What should we do with her? For her presence here may defile the sanctity of the Lord our God."[33] And the assembly said to the high priest, [Zachariah],[34] "Stand at the altar of the Lord, and pray about her. And whatever God reveals to you, that we shall do."

So the high priest, putting on the sacred vestment adorned with twelve bells,[35] entered the Holy of Holies. There he prayed about [Mary]. And—behold!—suddenly the angel of the Lord appeared before him, and said, "Zachariah, Zachariah[36], go out and call together all the men of the people whose wives have died[37]. Let each one bring with him a rod. And Mary shall become the wife of the one to whom God gives a sign, and she shall be entrusted to his care."[38]

And so messengers were sent out through all the region of Judea [to announce the decision of the high priest.] The trumpet of the Lord was sounded, and all the eligible men assembled.

31 In the Gospel of pseudo-Matthew, Mary's life in the temple is described in some detail. It states that each day should we pray until the third hour, then work from the third hour until the ninth hour, and then resume her prayer until an angel appeared to her bearing food. It states also that she was engaged in the work of spinning wool.

32 We also know that the age at which she left the service of the temple was at 12 years old. However the gospel of psuedomatthew says it could be around the age of 14, and in the discourse of Demetrius it is said at 15 years of age.

33 Presumably because she had reached the age of menstruation.

34 The identity of the high priest as Zachariah is revealed a little later. It has been inserted here for the sake of clarity.

35 See Exodus 28:33.

36 This is the same Zachariah the high priest who later will be the father of john the Baptist.

37 As stated by the apparition to Zachariah the priest, since he wanted all the old widows to be gathered, it must mean that saint Joseph the carpenter was an old widow. This further highlight that they were more looking for a guardian figure for her rather than a spouse. Something like the relationship between Esther and Mordecai in the book of Esther.

38 The gathering of staffs and awaiting a sign is similar to that happened at the time of Moses the prophet and those who contested Aaron. Aaron's staff alone sprouted.

CHAPTER 9

Now Joseph[39], [who was a carpenter,] put down his axe and went out on the way with the crowd [of men.] All of these gathered together [at the temple]. They went to the high priest, each one taking his rod with him. And the high priest took the rod from each of the men. He then entered the temple and prayed.

Once his prayer was complete, he took up all the rods once more and went out. But no sign had [yet] appeared in any of them. But when the high priest handed Joseph his rod, which was the last one, behold!—a dove sprang out from it. It flew up and alighted on Joseph's head.[40]

The high priest said to Joseph, "You are the one who has been chosen by Divine lot, that you should receive the Virgin of the Lord into your guardianship and protection." But Joseph resisted, saying, "But I have sons of my own[41]. And I am already an old man, whereas she is but a young girl. Hence I fear that I should appear ridiculous before the people of Israel!"

The high priest responded, "You should fear the Lord your God! Remember what God did to Dathan, Abiram and Korah[42], and how the earth opened up and swallowed them because they resisted His will.[43] Now fear God, O Joseph, lest the same thing happen to you and your household!"

And Joseph was afraid. So he took Mary into his charge. And he said to her, "Mary, see, I am taking you from the Temple of the Lord [into my own care and protection][44]. I must now leave you here in my house, while I myself go out to attend to my business as a carpenter. But I shall soon return to you. The Lord shall protect you!"[45]

39 Saint Joseph the carpenter is introduced abruptly highlighting that he is a well-known character to the audience.

40 In the doxology of St Joseph in the Coptic church there is a verse which states:

i *A dove appeared and rested in his rod, so Zacharias the priest gave her to him.*

In the Coptic tradition we compare the Virgin Mary to a pure dove, a symbol of purity. For this we exclaim:

ii *Hail to you Mary the beautiful dove, who gave birth to God the word for us. And*

iii *Hail to you mary the beautiful dove, full of wisdom, the mother of Jesus Christ.*

41 St Joseph also states that he has sons. This information is not well known and many people assumed that he was also a celibate character. However the statement that he has sons helps us understand why the jews believed that the lord had brothers (those that Joseph had from a previous marriage).

42 The incident with St Josephs staff is not mentioned in the gospels. The high priest seems to mention to Joseph that this is a decision taken by God and anything he does against this would be direct rebellion In other texts, it is said that they cast lots and the lot fell to Joseph.

43 See Numbers 16:31-33.

44 In the text the history of joseph the carpenter (*historia josephi fabri lignari*) this new testament apocrypha which is aimed at highlighting the perpetual virginity of st mary, states that the sons of st joseph were "judas, Justus, James and Simon".

45 The fact that they needed to take her into a guardian's care must have indicated that her parents had passed away at that point. Otherwise why would they need to entrust her to anyone.

CHAPTER 10

[SHORTLY AFTERWARDS] THERE WAS A MEETING OF THE PRIESTS. [At this meeting, the priests] resolved, "Let us make a veil for the Temple of the Lord." And the high priest said, "Call to me all the [seven] most faultless virgins[46] of the tribe of David [to make this veil.]" So [the officers of the temple] went forth to find seven such virgins. The high priest then recalled Mary, and that she was of the tribe of David, and also entirely without fault in the sight of God. [Thus it was that Mary was amongst the group of seven immaculate maidens of the tribe of David who were assembled to undertake the veil of the temple.]

And the high priest said, "Let us cast lots, to determine which of these maidens shall spin the gold thread, the white thread, the fine linen, the silk, the violet thread, the scarlet thread, and the thread of finest purple."[47] And it happened that Mary was chosen by lot to weave the fine purple and the scarlet. So she took them, and returned to her house [to perform the spinning and weaving].

Now in those days, Zachariah had been struck dumb,[48] so that a priest called Samuel was substituting for him [as high priest.] And Mary proceeded to spin with the thread of purple and the thread of scarlet[49].

46 The high priest here counts Mary among the virgins despite being betrothed to joseph and living in his house for a time, this highlights that it was an assumed guardianship rather than a physical marriage.

47 See Exodus 25:4.

48 This Zachariah is clearly identified with the father of St. John the Baptist, who was struck dumb before his son's birth. (See Luke 1:20.) The Coptic *Life of the Virgin Mary* specifies that Zachariah was a brother of Joachim. (Zachariah was struck dumb because he did not believe the angel which bore him the news of Elizabeth bearing a child, and as we know from the gospel of Luke that he will receive his voice back on the day that john is born).

49 It appears that Mary's link and work for the temple had not fully ceased since they still recall on her for the work of the veil.

CHAPTER 11

[Now, one day Mary] took the water-jar, and went forth to draw some water. And she suddenly heard the voice speak to her. It said, "Hail[50], you who are full of grace! The Lord is with you. Blessed are you among women." Mary [was greatly surprised,] and she looked around to right and left to see where the voice had come from. [But she saw no one there][51].

So, in astonishment, she went back into her house and put the water-jar down. Taking up the purple thread, she sat upon her chair and resumed her work with the spinning. And—behold!— an angel of the Lord appeared before her. It said, "Do not be afraid, O Mary, for you have found favor with the Lord of the whole universe! And you shall conceive a child by His Word." Upon hearing this, Mary pondered deeply within her heart, wondering to herself, "Is it possible that I shall conceive by the living God, and then give birth to a child in the manner of other women?"

The angel of the Lord replied [to her thoughts], "It shall not be [for you as it is with other women], Mary! For the Holy Spirit shall come over you, and the virtue of God will overshadow you. And therefore the One who is born of you shall be holy, and shall be called the Son of the Most High. And you are to give Him the name Jesus. He will save his people from their sins![52]

"And, behold, at this time your kinswoman Elizabeth has also conceived a son, although she is in her old age. She, whom people once called barren, is now in the sixth month [of her pregnancy]. For nothing is impossible with God!"[53]

And Mary said, "Behold, [I am] the handmaid of the Lord. Let it be done to me according to your word."

50 The words spoken by the angel *"hail, you who is full of grace, the lord is with you"* resonate with us in the Coptic church. The word used for hail is (xaire) which is more accurately translated rejoice. It is how we address the virgin Mary in many chants in the Coptic church whether in the (hitenis) in the liturgy or 'rashy ne' in praises.

   i   *"Hail to the handmaiden and mother, the virgin and the heaven, who carried in the flesh, He who sits upon the cherubim" (Wednesday theotokia)*

51 The idea of the angel appearing to her at a watering well is an uncommon one, however there is a church in Nazareth not far from where st Mary and st joseph lived that contains a well and they say this is the site of this first miraculous encounter. However, they are more likely to be at Jerusalem than Nazareth since the holy family only moved to Nazareth after their return from Egypt.

52 This is almost identical to the version of the annunciation seen in the gospel of st Luke, st Mary's response is almost word for word what is written in the gospel.

53 The text of this paragraph is present in the Neander/ Fabricius text, but not included in that of Tischendorf. It seems to be necessary as the motivation for Mary's visiting of Elizabeth, recounted in the next chapter.

CHAPTER 12

ONCE [MARY] HAD COMPLETED THE WORK WITH THE PURPLE AND scarlet thread, she took them and presented them to the high priest[54]. He blessed her and said, "O Mary, God has made you great and blessed, and you shall be blessed through all generations!"

And Mary, filled with exultation, went to her kinswoman Elizabeth, and knocked upon her door. When Elizabeth heard this, she went to the door and opened it. And [upon seeing Mary] she exclaimed, "How is it that the Mother of my Lord should visit me? [For as soon as you approached, the infant] which is inside of me leapt for joy and blessed you!"[55]

Now, the mysteries which the Archangel Gabriel had [previously] revealed [to her] were [at that time] kept hidden from Mary. So Mary turned her gaze to Heaven, and said, "Who am I that all generations should declare me blessed?"

As the days passed, [the child within her steadily grew] and her womb became larger. Struck with fear [that her pregnancy would be noticed], she returned to her house and hid herself inside from the people of Israel[56]. She was sixteen years old[57] when these mysterious things took place.

54 There is tradition that this curtain being made by the seven virgins is the same one that as torn from top to bottom on the day of crucifixion.

55 In this chapter is the famous encounter between the two, a summary of the events of what happened in the gospel of st Luke chapter 1.

56 In the Coptic church whenever we mention any glorification for the virgin saint Mary it is always associated with imagery of her pregnancy of God the word. For example, from the Wednesday Theotokia:

i *Great is the honor of Mary, above all the saints, for she was found worthy of receiving God the Word.*

ii *The one feared by the angels, Mary the virgin has carried in her Womb.*

How amazing is it that we glorify her in such a manner, however being put in the situation of being found pregnant must have been a traumatic and embarrassing event for St Mary, so much so that she returned to her house and hid herself.

57 Here we are told that St Mary was 16 years old, having lived in the house of St Joseph for at least 4 years. Yet as we will see they still did not expect that she would be pregnant, thus she was struck with fear that her pregnancy would be noticed.

CHAPTER 13

[THUS MARY KEPT HER PREGNANCY SECRET UNTIL SHE] REACHED the sixth month. But then, Joseph [one day] came back from his business and entered his house. And—behold!—he noticed that [Mary] was clearly pregnant.[58] [In shock and sadness,] he struck his face and cast himself down upon the sackcloth. Weeping bitterly, he said, "How shall I look upon the Lord my God? And what prayer am I to make for this maiden? For I accepted her as a virgin from the Temple of the Lord God, but I have failed to protect her! Who is it that has played me false? Who is it that has inflicted this evil upon my household, and defiled this virgin? Is this not a repetition of what happened to Adam? For when Adam was occupied in prayer, the serpent entered and found Eve alone and then deceived her. And thus it has befallen me also!"

Then Joseph arose from the ground. He took Mary and said to her, "You were cared for by God so dearly! Why have you done such a thing? Have you completely forgotten the Lord your God—you, who were once led into the Holy of Holies? Why have you disgraced yourself—you, who received food from the very hand of an angel?"[59]

Mary wept bitterly. She protested, "I am pure; I have had no relations with any man!" But Joseph retorted, "How is it then that you have an infant growing in your womb?" Mary answered, "As the Lord my God lives, truly I do not know how this has come about."[60]

58 Here we have a much more animated recantation of the events written in the gospels when st joseph noticed St Mary's pregnancy. I am sure it must have been very difficult for st joseph to understand and just like in the gospel it is obvious that st Mary did not try and explain the annunciation but rather waited for God to justify her.

59 Saint Joseph being a righteous man, must have been troubled at the sight of saint Mary's pregnancy. The text also highlights that he was away for some time at work, and that saint Mary herself was away helping her cousin Elizabeth, this may have increased his suspicion and doubt, therefore it was imperative that he receive a definitive vision/answer about what to do, as we will see in the next chapter.

60 Similarly, st Mary did not mention this to anyone but just like the gospel says, 'she kept all these things in her heart.' However, as we will see in the next chapter, she may have mentioned the news of the miraculous annunciation as Joseph ponders that this may in fact be miraculous.

CHAPTER 14

JOSEPH WAS ASTONISHED [BOTH AT MARY'S PREGNANCY, AND HER sincere assertion of her virginity.] So he pondered deeply[61] and wondered, "What am I to do?" And Joseph said to himself, "If I conceal her sin, I myself shall be guilty according to the law of the Lord. But if I reveal [what has happened] and hand her over to the people of Israel, I fear, lest I commit an injustice by giving her innocent blood over to the sentence of death. For, indeed, the child within her may really be from an angel. What, then, am I to do with her?" [After considering thus, at last he came to a decision,] resolving to himself, "I will divorce her in secret."

Night came upon [Joseph, and he went to bed and slept.] And— behold!—the angel of the Lord appeared to him in his dreams. It said, "Do not be afraid to take this maiden as your wife! For the child that is within her is of the Holy Spirit. She will give birth to a Son, and you shall give Him the name Jesus. And he shall save his people from their sins." And Joseph arose from sleep and glorified the God of Israel, who had granted him this wonderful privilege[62]. And he continued to keep and protect [Mary.][63]

61 Another animated version of the thoughts of Saint Joseph. The fact that it is written in such an animated way may highlight that this is what was circulating around in spoken tradition.

62 The apparition of the angel here is almost identical to that of the encounter in the gospel. However here is added that joseph arose and glorified God who had granted him this wonderful privilege.

63 The Coptic church refers to St Joseph as the keeper/protector of the secret of incarnation, this may be derived from the last verse and he continued to keep and protect her.

CHAPTER 15

[AROUND THAT TIME,] THE SCRIBE ANNAS[64] CAME TO VISIT JOSEPH. He said to him, "Joseph, why is it that you have not appeared at the synagogue [in recent times]?" Joseph replied that he had been wearied with his travels, and so had been taking his rest.[65]

But the scribe turned about, and saw that Mary was pregnant. He rushed off to the [high] priest, and told him, "This man Joseph, to whose character you once gave witness, has committed a dreadful sin!" And the [high] priest asked, "What is this [you are talking about]?" [Annas] replied, "He has defiled the virgin whom he received from the temple of the Lord! He has married her in secret, and not revealed it to the people of Israel." The high priest [was perplexed] and asked, "Has Joseph really done this thing?" The scribe Annas replied, "Send your officers to investigate, and they shall find that she is indeed pregnant!"

The officers went off, and they found everything exactly as [Annas] had said. So they led [Mary] together with Joseph before the tribunal [of the priests.][66] And the [high] priest said to Mary, "Why have you disgraced your soul in this manner? Have you forgotten the Lord your God—you, who were once led into the Holy of Holies; you, who were once fed by the hand of an angel? Indeed, you have heard the hymns of praise [of the angels] and danced in the sight of God Himself! Why have you done this [terrible thing]?"

64 Annas the scribe comes to ask about Joseph, where he finds St Mary pregnant. However, upon discovering Mary's pregnancy he is troubled and delivers this information to the high priest. Why was he so troubled if Mary was pregnant being betrothed to joseph and living in his house all these years? Maybe it was because it was widely understood that the "marriage was more of a guardianship than a conjugal union".

65 In the doxology for St Joseph the Carpenter we say:

i *The lord chose joseph with a heavenly sign to take care of the virgin in his house.*

ii *Joseph doubted her virginity, the angel announced to him, o joseph son of David.*

iii *Do not fear to take Mary as your wife, for the one whom she bears, is of the holy spirit.*

iv *Mary is the treasure, that joseph brought, and he found the jewel that was hidden within.*

66 We see that the high priest reprimands both joseph and Mary and has ignored their claim of innocence. How difficult this must be for a young girl at a tender age of 16, to be accused of such a sin in the mist of all these priests.

[Upon hearing these reproaches, Mary] wept bitterly. She exclaimed, "As the Lord my God lives, I am pure in the sight of the Lord. I have never had relations with any man!"

Then the [high] priest [turned his attention] to Joseph, and said to him, "What is this thing you have done?" But Joseph replied, "As the Lord my God lives, I am guiltless; I have never had conjugal relations with her." The [high] priest reprimanded him, saying, "Do not give false witness, but speak the truth! For you have certainly married her by stealth, and not disclosed it to the people of Israel. And you have not bowed your head to the almighty hand [of God], so that your offspring should be blessed." But Joseph remained silent.[67]

67 This text delves deeper into the feelings and emotions
   that may have occurred during this time. As opposed to
   the gospels factual approach.

CHAPTER 16

THE [HIGH] PRIEST [AGAIN] SPOKE TO JOSEPH. "RESTORE THE virgin whom you have accepted from the Temple of the Lord!", he said. [When he heard this,] Joseph poured out tears profusely. Then the priest said to him, "I shall give you [both] the Lord's water of testing to drink. And it shall reveal before your eyes whether or not [either of] you have sinned."[68] And so the priest took the water [of testing] and gave it to Joseph to drink. He then sent him away into the hill country [for a period of time. Joseph] returned from [this trial] completely unharmed. He then [similarly] gave Mary the water [of testing] to drink, and sent her forth into the hill country[69]. She likewise returned unharmed.[70]

All the people were amazed that no sin had been revealed [in either Joseph or Mary.] And the high priest declared, "God Himself has made manifest your [innocence from] sin[71]. It is not I who judge you; rather it is [the Lord Himself] who has absolved you!" And Joseph took Mary and together they went home, rejoicing greatly and giving glory to the God of Israel.[72]

68 This "water of testing" apparently corresponds with what is described in Numbers 5. In that chapter, the drinking of specially consecrated water is prescribed as a means of determining questions of sexual fidelity.

69 In the Coptic church we do not have any reference to this, however being tied to old Jewish traditions written in the Torah, there is little doubt in its authenticity.

70 The fact that both Mary and Joseph return from the hill country unharmed, after having drunk the water of testing, indicated that both were entirely innocent, i.e. that Joseph had not had conjugal relations with Mary, and that Mary has had no relations with Joseph or any other man.

71 The response that "God himself has made manifest your innocence from sin" spoken by the high priest is an admission that both are guiltless and thus that there must be something miraculous at play.

72 In the Old Testament the punishment of adultery is death. The fact that both Joseph and Mary passed this trial, may have very well saved them from a public scrutiny and violence.

CHAPTER 17

[A SHORT TIME AFTERWARDS] A DECREE WAS ISSUED BY THE emperor Augustus Caesar [that a census should be taken of all the population, with each person being enrolled according to their town of origin. Therefore, it was required] that all who were of the town of Bethlehem [should return to that town] and be enrolled there. And Joseph said [to himself], "I will ensure that my sons are enrolled. But what should I do about this maiden [Mary]? How will I enroll her? Shall I declare her to be my wife? I should blush to do that [since she is not really my wife, but entrusted, as a virgin, to my guardianship.] Or shall I declare her to be my daughter? But all the Israelites know that she is not, [in fact,] my daughter. Well! I shall do whatever the Lord wills me to do, on the day of the Lord."[73]

And Joseph saddled a she-donkey and had [Mary] sit upon it[74]. [The couple set out on the journey to Bethlehem. And two of the sons of Joseph,] Jose and Simon,[75] followed at a distance of about three miles.

[At a certain point in the journey,] Joseph turned back and saw that [Mary] appeared to be sorrowful. And he thought to himself, "Perhaps the infant which is inside her is causing her this sorrow." But at another time, he turned back and saw that she was laughing. And he said to her, "O Mary, what is happening to you, that I see your face sometimes joyful and sometimes filled with sadness?" Mary replied to Joseph, "It is because I see two groups of people with my eyes—one is weeping and sorrowful, while the other group is laughing and exulting."[76]

73 The sense of this comment is that Joseph, while not making a decision, commits himself to doing whatever is the will of the Lord at the time.

74 This is the beginning of the Christmas story. As st Mary and the holy family are led to Bethlehem to be registered.

75 These two are identified as 'brothers of Jesus' (i.e. sons of Joseph), in Mark 6:3. Here we have direct mention of josephs sons by name, those being attributed as brothers of Jesus.

76 The Gospel of pseudo-Matthew adds an explanation of this vision; namely that the people who are weeping are the Jews who do not accept Christ, and the people who are rejoicing are the Gentiles who accept Jesus as their Savior.

When they were about halfway through the journey, Mary said, "Joseph, take me down from this donkey. For the infant within me urges now that he is [very soon] due to be born![77]" [Joseph accordingly] removed her from the back of the donkey. He said to her [anxiously], "Where am I to take you to preserve your modesty [in giving birth to the child]? For this is a deserted place."

77 Mary here starts to feel the beginning of labor pain. In the Thursday theotokia we mention:

i   *Upon her head was a crown of twelve stars, she being with child cried out in labor, and in pain to give birth.*

CHAPTER 18

[JOSEPH LOOKED AROUND FOR A SAFE PLACE WHERE MARY MIGHT give birth to her infant. And,] finding a cave[78], he led her into it. He left his two sons with her, and went forth himself to find a Hebrew midwife in the region of Bethlehem.

Joseph related [that at this time],[79] "As I walked, I looked upwards and saw the vault of the sky, the Heavens, and the winds. And they were standing [completely] still. And even the birds of Heaven [seemed to have stopped] in the middle of their flight! At looking at the earth, I saw there a dish of food placed on the ground and a group of workmen reclining about it. Their hands were in the dish [as if taking food, but completely motionless]. And those who [seemed to be eating] did not eat, and those [who seemed to be] raising their hands did not raise their hands, and those who [seemed to be bringing food to their mouth] did not bring food to their mouths. Rather, all had their faces turned upwards, fixed [motionlessly] at the Heavens. And the sheep, which [seemed to be] going forth, remained perfectly still. And the shepherd, [who seemed to be] raising his staff to goad them with it, [remained completely immobile] with his hand suspended in the air. And, looking upon the course of a river, I saw there goats with their mouths over the water [as if they were drinking]. But they did not drink. Indeed, at that moment it was is if all things had stopped in their course, [rendered completely immobile!]"

78 The fact that Christ is born in a cave is a new notion. However, doing some research it was found that animals were more likely stored in a cave rather than a barn which was constructed with hard-to-find wood.

79 The dramatic effect of change of narration to the point of view of joseph is highlighted in this chapter as according to joseph the world stood still at the moment of Christ's birth.

CHAPTER 19

[AND JOSEPH CONTINUED HIS NARRATION THUS:][80]

"And then suddenly I saw a woman descending from the mountains. She asked me, 'Sir, where are you going?' And I replied, 'I am looking for a Hebrew midwife.' She enquired, 'Are you of the people of Israel then?' And I said, 'Yes, indeed.' She said, 'And who is that woman who is giving birth to a child in the cave?' I told her the she was my betrothed. She asked me, 'But is she not your wife?' I told her, 'She is Mary, who was raised in the Holy of Holies in the Temple of the Lord! She was entrusted [to my guardianship by] lot, and is [therefore] not my wife. The child which she bears was conceived of the Holy Spirit!'"

The woman asked him, "Is that [really] true?" Joseph said to her, "Come and see for yourself." And the midwife and Joseph went together to the cave. And—behold!—a glowing cloud shone around the cave. The midwife exclaimed, "My soul rejoices today! For my eyes have seen a marvelous thing, for today salvation is born to the people of Israel." And suddenly the cloud vanished from the cave and a great light appeared, [of such intense brightness] that their eyes could scarcely endure it.[81]

But little by little the light faded away, so that they could see the [new-born] infant. And the baby suckled at the bosom of his mother, Mary[82]. The midwife cried out, saying, "This is a great day for me, for I have beheld this wondrous sight!"

The midwife then went out of the cave, and Salome[83], [who happened to be walking by,] met her.[84] And the midwife, [who knew Salome,] said to her, "I have a strange thing to relate to you. A virgin has given birth to a Son, something which nature itself does not allow!" But Salome [was incredulous, and] said "As my Lord God lives, unless I can test [her virginity] with my finger[85], I will not believe that she who has given birth is [really] a virgin!"

80   The Greek text for this chapter given in the Tischendorf edition differs significantly from that of the Papyrus Bodmer 5 manuscript. Since the text of the Tischendorf edition is clearer and more complete, it has been followed in the present translation. This same comment applies also in Chapters 20 and 21.

81   Saint Joseph here explains to the midwife the situation, that St Mary is his betrothed and not his wife, and that she has conceived by the Holy Spirit. Followed by the cloud and light that filled the place and the lack of use of the midwife as when she had arrived the child was suckling already. In the Thursday Theotokia there is a verse which states:

  i   *"For He who was born is God, born without pain from the father, and He was also born according to the flesh, without pain for the virgin"*.

In contrast to the passage in the chapter above, the two seemingly contradictory, however this chapter explains that St Mary first felt birth contractions (labor pain) however delivered on her own without pain (or need for a midwife), as the delivery did not loosen her virginity.

82   In the Coptic chantings of Kiahk and in the praise of Monday Theotokia we say, "He drank milk from your chest, the creator of all lives, you carried him in your bosom, Maria ti Parthenos."

83   Here we are introduced to Salome. In the Coptic tradition and in the famous kiahk praises we say "Salome witnessed that the virgin has given birth". We shall see in the next chapter the dramatic events that occur as Salome tries to confirm this virginal birth.

84   The Gospel of pseudo-Matthew identifies this Salome as a midwife also. Fabricius suggests that this Salome is same woman mentioned in Matthew 20:20, Mark 15:40, John 19:25, who was (according to tradition) a sister of Mary and the mother of the apostles James and John.

CHAPTER 20

AND SO THE MIDWIFE [TOGETHER WITH SALOME[86]] ENTERED [THE cave. The midwife] said to Mary, "Recline yourself, for a great test is awaiting you!" And then Salome put forward her finger[87] [in such a way to test whether Mary was really a virgin. After doing this,] she suddenly rushed out, saying, "Woe is me, for I have been irreverent and faithless! Indeed, I have presumed to test the living God Himself! And now my hand [which did this wicked thing] is dropping off from me, as if scalded with fire!"

And she knelt before the Lord, and prayed, "O God of my ancestors, remember me! Remember that I am of the seed of Abraham, Isaac and Jacob. Do not betray [my guilt] to the people of Israel, but restore me [to the privacy and obscurity] of the poor. O Lord, you know that everything which I have done I have done in Your Name, in order that I may receive a just recompense for You!"

And the angel of the Lord appeared to her and said, "Salome, the Lord has heard your prayer! Reach out to the child, and hold Him in your arms. He shall be to you your salvation and your delight!" And Salome approached the child filled with joy. And she said to herself, "How shall I embrace [such a sacred infant?"[88] And at once her heart urged her to worship Him, and she declared, "A great King has been born to Israel!" She was then instantaneously healed [from the burning pain which afflicted her hand]. And she went forth from the cave, having been forgiven for her sins.

And—behold!—a voice was heard, saying, "Salome, Salome, do not speak of this miraculous thing which you have witnessed, until the child has entered into Jerusalem."

85 Thomas the apostle has also used the same vow "unless I put my finger in his side I will not believe"

86 In the Coptic Kiahk chanting's we mention Salome often, for example, apart from the verse mentioned above, a passage in the fourth explanation of amba Marcos states; "Salome was attending with the carpenter, the blessed elder joseph.." referring to this blessed night.

87 This story about the virgin Mary being tested by Salome was apparent in the early church, as there is mention of it by st clement of Alexandria in his stromata.

88 In this chapter we have Salome trying to test Mary's virginity and suffering immense pain in her arm, followed by the angelic apparition which tells her to hold the child who will save her. In this way, Salome testifies to the virginal birth and the Christ who will save his people from their sins.

CHAPTER 21

[SHORTLY AFTER MARY HAD GIVEN BIRTH,] JOSEPH MADE preparations to go into Judea. [Now, at that time] a great tumult had arisen in Bethlehem, for Magi had come [from the eastern lands], asking, "Where is He who has been born to be King of the Jews?[89] For we have seen His star in the east[90], and now we come to pay Him homage."

When [King] Herod heard of this, he was greatly agitated. He sent his officers to the Magi. And he summoned the high priests to himself, and asked them, "What is written of the [prophesied] King, who is called the Messiah? Where is he to be born?" And they replied, "In Bethlehem, in Judea. For thus it is written [in the Scriptures]."[91]

[Herod then] dismissed the high priests, and questioned the Magi. He said to them, "What sign have you seen concerning this new-born King? Speak to me [plainly.]" And the Magi said to him, "An immensely great star has arisen, more radiant than all the other stars of Heaven. [It is so bright that all the other stars] cannot be seen. And thus we have come to know that a great King has been born to Israel. We have come here to pay Him our homage."

Herod said to them, "Go forth and seek Him. And if you find Him, inform me, so that I myself may go and pay Him homage." And the Magi [accordingly] went forth. And—behold!—the star which they had seen in the eastern skies led their way, until they came to a certain cave. And there, the star stood still above the cave.

And [the Magi] saw there the infant and Mary, his mother.[92] [And they fell to their knees and paid homage to him.] Opening

89 It is important to note that, the presence of the magi made such a commotion for they were very dignified and came as an envoy rather than three single men as is depicted in many pictures of the nativity.

90 The Magi where traditionally thought of as descendants of Balaam and the prophesy about the star is mentioned in numbers 24:17 "I see him, but not now; I behold him, but not nigh; a star shall come forth out of Jacob, and a scepter shall rise out of isreal.."

91 This story is also mentioned in the second chapter of the book of Matthew.

92 In the hymn of Friday Theotokia we also say, "He adorned mary with His advent, and fulfilled the prophecies, the Magi came and worshiped Him: with precious gifts they were introduced."

their bags, they brought forth gold and frankincense and myrrh,[93] [humbly offering these as gifts and tributes to the child.]

Then, having been warned by an angel that they should not return to Judea, they made their way back to their native land by another route.

93 The exact same gifts are mentioned as the gospels and
similarly the angelic vision which tells them to go home
some other way. In the Thursday theotokia:

i *"They offered Him, frankincense for He is God, gold
for He is king, and myrrh as a sign of His life-giving
death".*

CHAPTER 22

WHEN HEROD CAME TO REALIZE THAT HE HAD BEEN DISOBEYED by the Magi, he was furious. He sent forth executioners, commanding them to put to death all male children [in Bethlehem] who were two years of age or younger[94]. When Mary heard of this slaughter of children, she was struck with terror. She took her child and wrapped Him in swaddling cloth [to conceal Him][95]. And she kept Him in a stable containing oxen[96].

[Meanwhile,] Elizabeth [also] heard that [the soldiers of Herod were killing male children, and that therefore] her son John was being sought after[97]. So she hurried forth into the hill country, and looked for a place in which to conceal him. But she found no suitable hiding place. [Overcome by anguish,] she wept and cried out, "O Mountain of God, accept both me, the mother, and my son [into your care]![98]" And she could not rise up, for very fear. And suddenly the mountainside opened up, and received [Elizabeth and the infant John] into the cleft! And a great light shone forth around them [as they hid in the cavern in the mountainside], for the angel of the Lord was with them, keeping watch over them.

94 This is the famous slaughter of the children of Bethlehem. In the fifth explanation of Anba Marcos we say,

   i   *"Herod the king was confused, from his fear he ordered the death, of all the baby boys, living in and around Bethlehem."*

95 The swaddling cloth is how mothers wrap babies so that they limit movement. In many icons they draw baby Jesus wrapped like this but with burial material signifying his death and burial in a cave prior to the resurrection.

96 Here we are told Mary hides the baby Jesus in a manger with oxen, until their escape to Egypt.

97 John the Baptist at this time is around six months of age. He then is definitely within the age group of the children that Herod is seeking to kill. Furthermore as we will see in the next chapter Herod was specifically looking for John, especially because the events of his miraculous birth were known.

98 This story of the mountain accepting Elizabeth and baby John is not commonly known, however in tradition it explains that they stayed there for the rest of their lives until john started proclaiming repentance and baptism. In the Coptic tradition we say that john was raised by angels and that they taught him to proclaim repentance and to identify the Christ when he sees the epiphany.

CHAPTER 23

BUT HEROD CONTINUED TO SEARCH FOR JOHN [IN ORDER TO KILL him.][99] And he sent his officers to Zachariah, [his father], who was standing at the altar [at that time. The officers questioned him,] saying, "Where have you hidden your son?" But he answered them, saying, "I am a priest in the service of God, and I abide here within the Temple of the Lord. How, then, should I know where my son may be now?"

The officers then left him and went and related all this to Herod. And Herod was filled with wrath. He declared, "His son is destined to rule over Israel!" So he sent forth [his officers] to Zacharias once more. [Herod instructed his officers to say to Zacharias, "Speak the truth! Where is your son [hidden]? Do you not realize that your life's blood lies in my hands?" And the officers went forth, and said all this to Zacharias.

But he responded, "As God is my witness, I don't know where my son is! If you wish, go ahead and shed my blood. For God shall receive my spirit, for it will be innocent blood that you spill in the forecourt [of the altar] in the Temple of the Lord." And [so it was that,] at the dawning of day, Zachariah was killed.[100]

But, [as these things had happened within the privacy of the temple,] the people of Israel did not [yet] know that he had been slain.[101]

99 This statement suggests that Herod mistakenly believed that John was the child who had been born to be king, of whom the Magi spoke. This may have resulted from John's birth being so widely known in the community.

100 See Matthew 23:35

101 This is the murder of Zachariah the priest the father of John the Baptist. Whether this may be the person referred to by the Lord Jesus in the gospel where he reprimands the Jews saying "that all the righteous blood shed from the righteous Abel to Zachariah son of Berechiah..." is not known since Zachariah is such a popular name.

CHAPTER 24.

When it was the time of salutation,[102] the priests began to leave [the temple]. But Zachariah did not come out to meet them to give them a blessing, as was the customary practice. And so the priests all stood waiting for him to bid them farewell and to bless [God] the Most High.

When [Zachariah] did not appear, they became afraid[103]. But one of them dared to enter[104] [into the sanctuary.] He saw congealed blood lying beside the altar. And he heard a voice, saying, "Zachariah has been slain. And his blood shall not be wiped away until his avenger comes!"

When he heard this, the priest was afraid. He rushed out and told the other priests what he had witnessed. When they heard this, they all went in [to the sanctuary], and saw what had taken place. And the panels of the Temple began to groan[105], while [the priests, in anguish,] tore their garments from top to bottom.[106] The body [of Zachariah] was nowhere to be found. But his blood, which lay upon the forecourt [of the altar] in the temple, was transformed into the likeness of stone.

The priests went out from the temple, all trembling with horror. They announced to the people that Zachariah [the high priest] had been murdered. When the tribes of the people heard this news, they lamented deeply. And they mourned for him for some three days and three nights.

After these three days had passed, the priests held a meeting about whom they should appoint in his place [as high priests. Lots were cast,] and the lot fell to Simeon[107]. He indeed was the one who had been told by an oracle of the Holy Spirit that he should not see death until he had beheld Christ in the flesh.[108]

102 That is, the time at which the priests finished their daily duties and departed from the temple. It was evidently the custom for them to receiving a salutation and blessing from the high priest (i.e. Zachariah) at that time.

103 In the beginning when Zachariah lingered in the altar and did not come out, it is reminiscent of the situation when he lingered in the alter after the vision of the angel letting him know about the birth of john. However, this time he was murdered for supposedly hiding his own child.

104 Only the high priest is permitted to enter this area and thus the scripture notes that one of the priests dared to enter.

105 The book of Amos 8:3 states a prophesy "and the ceiling panels of the temple shall wail in that day"

106 In the Greek text given in the Neander and Fabricius editions, it is the panels themselves which are torn from top to bottom.

107 Now Simeon the elder was selected as high priest instead of Zachariah, this is the man who we read about in the gospel saying "lord you are now letting your servant depart in peace according to your word…."

108 See Luke 2:25.

CHAPTER 25.

It is I, James[109], who have written this history. After a tumult had arisen in Jerusalem following the death of Herod, I went forth into the desert until the agitation in Jerusalem had subsided. [And it was while I was in the desert that I wrote this account.][110]

I give glory to God, who has given me the wisdom to write this narration for you, [my readers,] who are spiritual and fear God. May grace be with all those who revere our Lord Jesus Christ, to whom be all glory and honor forever and ever! Amen.[111]

109 There seems to be a bit of contention and skepticism that saint James the less wrote this around 4 AD after the death of Herod. Furthermore, it was not believed that he wrote this while the lord was still a child. Nevertheless it is seen that we derive a lot of our belief about st Mary and the nativity from this recount.

110 Although the text enclosed in square brackets is not in the original, this seems to be the implied significance of that author's recounting that he had taken refuge into the desert.

111 The Coptic church loves the Virgin Mary so much that on any given Sunday during the midnight chantings (tasbeha), the name Mary is mentioned seventy times.

www.ingramcontent.com/pod-product-compliance
Lightning Source LLC
Chambersburg PA
CBHW031934080426
42734CB00007B/689